My Amazing Toddler Behavioral Series

I Wash My Hands.
I Say Bye-Bye
GERMS!

An Affirmation-Themed Toddler
Book About Germs (Ages 2-4)

By
Suzanne T. Christian

TWO RAVENS
BOOKS

Two Little Ravens
CHILDREN'S NON-FICTION BOOKS

Paperback Edition: 9781964202686
Hardcover Edition: 9781964202693
Digital Edition: 9781964202709

Published in the United States by Two Ravens Books LLC,
254 Chapman Rd, Ste 209, Newark DE 19702

'Expand the mind, free the imagination, one title at a time.'
www.tworavensbooks.com

Welcome to

I Wash My Hands.
I Say Bye-Bye Germs!

This engaging illustrated book has cheerful, easy-to-understand affirmations that help young children build healthy hygiene habits through fun and repetition.

As you read together, your child will learn when and why to wash their hands in an empowering, non-scary way.

Each page features playful rhymes and familiar scenarios, such as snack time, playtime, and potty breaks, designed to make handwashing part of your toddler's daily routine.

Through repetition and encouragement, your little one will gain confidence and independence while learning to say, "Bye-bye, germs!"

Prepare for a joyful, educational journey into hand hygiene, self-care, and positive habits, one bubbly wash at a time!

Suzanne T. Christian

Germs are like tiny bugs that sneak and play. I wash my hands to chase them away!

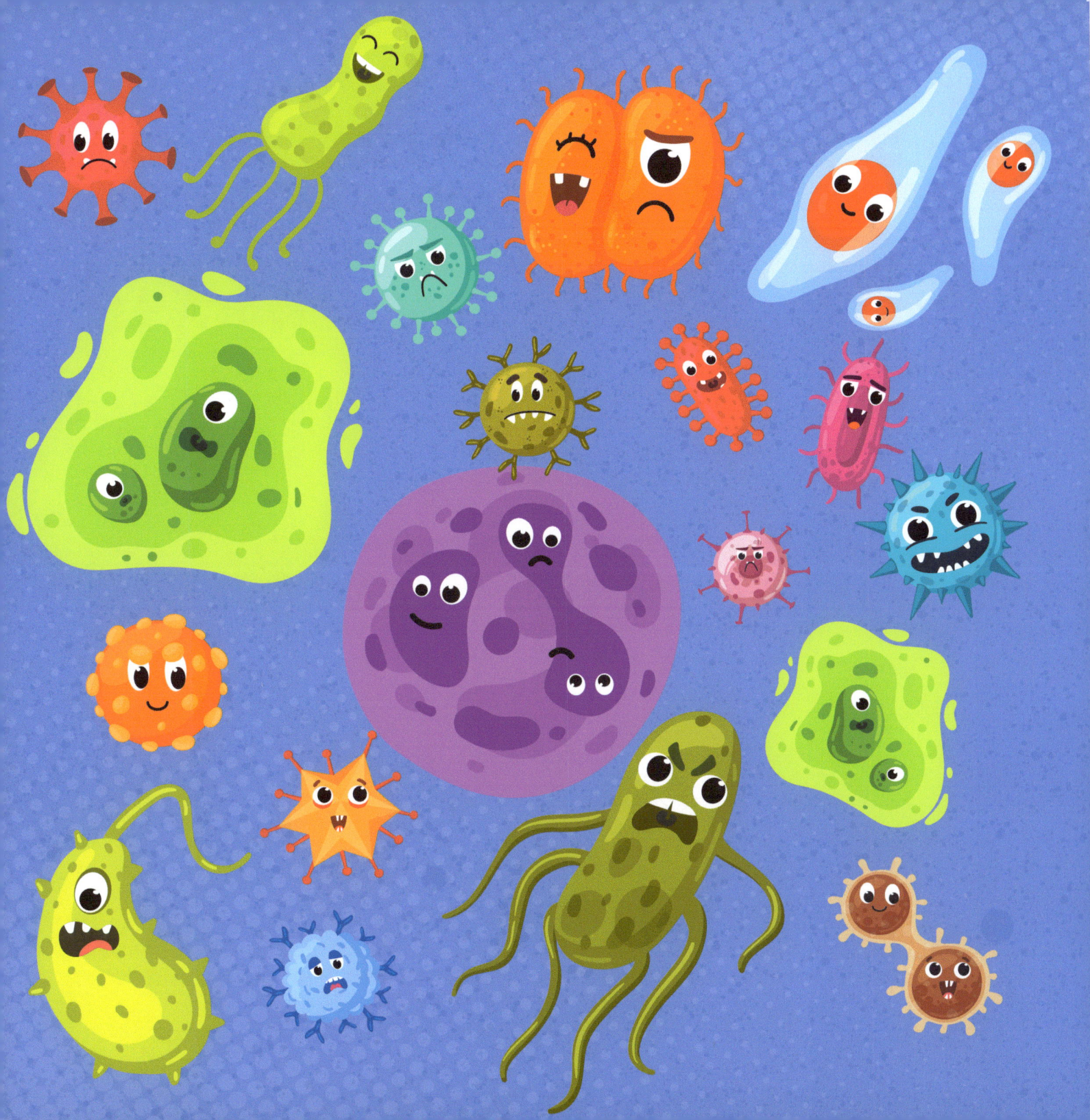

When I get home
from school or play,
I wash my hands;
I say bye-bye
germs!

Before I eat my
yummy snack,
I wash my hands,

pat, pat, pat!

Potty time is all done;
washing hands is so much fun!

If I touch the floor before I eat my snack, I wash my hands; then I come back!

After blowing my
little nose,
I wash my hands,
and away germs go!

When I cough or sneeze,
I wash my hands;
I say bye-bye germs!

After I play with my furry friend,
I wash my hands from end to end!

Sharing toys is nice to do; washing hands is important too!

After touching
buttons or doors,
I wash my hands,
germs no more!

When I sneeze, a lot can fly;

ah choo!

I wash my hands so
germs say bye-bye!

I wash my hands after making a mess with glue; that's what I do!

Germs can hide even when my hands look clean, so I wash in between!

WATER AND SOAP

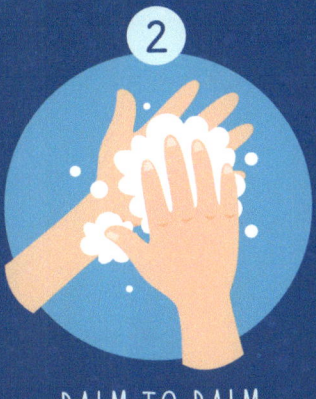

PALM TO PALM

I wash my hands both front and back, and between my fingers. **Pita-Pat-Pat!**

BETWEEN FINGERS

WASH WRISTS

BACK OF HANDS

WASH THUMBS

When I dig in dirt and sand,
I wash my hands!

If I pick up something yucky,
I wash my hands,
scrub-a-dub, so bubbly!

After a day at the park,
I wash my hands before dark!

I Wash My Hands.
I Say Bye-Bye
GERMS!
The End!

My Amazing Toddler Behavioral Series

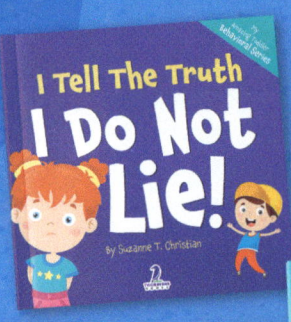

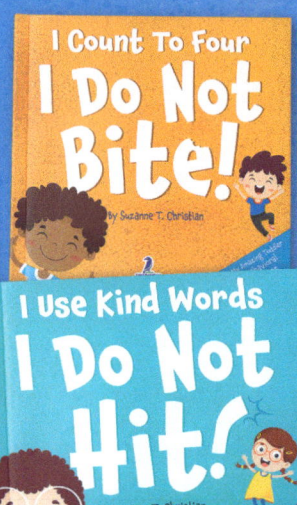

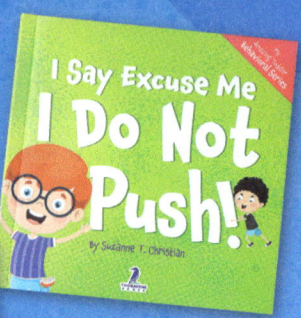

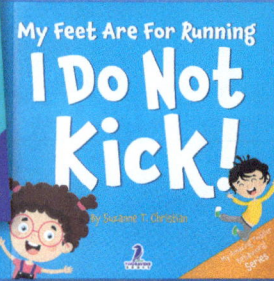

Check Out
Suzanne T. Christian's beloved series
'My Amazing Toddler Behavioral Series'.
Young readers are sure to enjoy!

Two Little Ravens

CHILDREN'S NON-FICTION BOOKS

Dear Amazing Reader,

Thank you for diving into **I Wash My Hands. I Say Bye-Bye Germs!** with me. If this book touched your heart or made a difference for a young reader, I'd be grateful if you could share your thoughts in a review. Your feedback inspires my future work and helps others discover the magic within these pages.

I'd love to hear from you directly if you have suggestions or ideas for improving the book. Please feel free to reach out to me at **suzanne.christian@tworavensbooks.com.** Your voice counts, and I cherish it deeply.

With heartfelt gratitude,

www.ingramcontent.com/pod-product-compliance
Lightning Source LLC
Chambersburg PA
CBHW041445120626
46547CB00002B/351